A Plan
for
Stewardship Education
and
Development
through the Year

DAVID W. GORDON

Morehouse Publishing
NEW YORK • HARRISBURG • DENVER

Morehouse Publishing, 4775 Linglestown Road, Harrisburg, PA 17112

Morehouse Publishing, 445 Fifth Avenue, New York, NY 10016

Morehouse Publishing is an imprint of Church Publishing Incorporated.
www.churchpublishing.org

Library of Congress Cataloging-in-Publication Data
Gordon, David W. (David Walter). 1927-
    A plan for stewardship education and development through the year
    / David W. Gordon.
       p. cm.
    ISBN 978-0-8192-1803-2 (pbk.)
    1. Stewardship. Christian—Study and teaching. 2. Episcopal Church —Education. I. Title.
BV722.G59 1998   98-44028
248'.6'071—dc21   CIP

Printed in the United States of America

Contents

Glossary

Congregations within denominations other than the Episcopal Church may find the following glossary of terminology used throughout the manual useful:

"Rector" or "Vicar" refers to the clergyperson in charge of a congregation.

"Vestry" or "Bishop's Committee" refers to the (elected or selected) governing body of the local congregation.

"Senior Warden" is the title of the lay person who heads the local church's governing body.

"Parish" or "Mission" are titles for individual churches.

"Diocese" represents a geographical cluster of local congregations (parishes/missions).

"Province" refers to a geographical cluster of dioceses.

"The national church" refers to the Episcopal Church in the U.S.A.

"Annual Meeting" is the yearly business meeting of the local congregation.

"Synod" refers to the annual meeting of a Province.

"General Convention" is the triennial meeting of the national Episcopal Church.

"The Anglican Communion" is the term used to describe the relationship of churches throughout the world which trace their roots to the Church of England.

Foreword

The plan presented in this manual has three goals:

    1) to introduce a broader and deeper understanding of Christian Stewardship;
    2) to offer guidance for the implementation of that understanding;
    3) to emphasize that Christian Stewardship is to be a matter of concern throughout the year.

The manual has been designed primarily for use in local churches, but the basic principles and techniques are also applicable to other levels of church administration (i.e., Diocese, Deanery, Region, District, etc.).

Many of the ideas and materials contained in the manual are original. The rest evolve from a variety of methods and materials utilized during over thirty years of parish ministry and nearly ten and one-half years as Director of Stewardship for the Episcopal Diocese of New York. The basic framework for the program is an adaptation of the DISC (Dimensions in Stewardship Commitment) program, developed in the Presbyterian Church around thirty years ago, and introduced in the Episcopal Diocese of California in 1971.

As of the time of the printing of this edition of the manual, the program has been presented in diocesan stewardship conferences and other meetings in forty-two dioceses of the Episcopal Church, three dioceses of the Anglican Church of Canada, and the Diocese of Nassau and the Bahamas. Around 350 congregations within the same dioceses had received individual "shepherding" while using the manual. Results have been significant, with churches reporting major increases in their numbers of pledges and in the dollar amounts pledged, as well as in the numbers of additional people who are participating in the life of the parish in general.

Dioceses, parishes, missions, or individuals who may desire additional information or assistance regarding the manual or the program, are invited to contact The Rev. David W. Gordon, 130 Avenida Barbera, Sonoma, CA 95476. Telephone: (707) 935-1031.

Appreciation is due friends and colleagues who have offered constructive criticism, representatives of other denominations who have provided moral support and encouragement, and to my own family members and former congregations who have demonstrated an attitude of Christian Stewardship through the years. Editorial assistance has been received from Mr. John Gordon, Rev. Beatrice Blair (deceased), Mr. A. Wallace Owen (deceased), Mrs. Gloria Norman, Rev. Robert Grafe, Rev. Richard Sloan, and Rev. Richard Jones.

—DWG

Introduction

The word "stewardship" seems to cause most people to think "money." A church which is experiencing financial problems is often told, "Work on your stewardship." Many congregations appear to think of Stewardship as fund-raising, and the subject is rarely raised except during a comparatively brief flurry of activity at budget-building time. The annual stewardship sermon and some sort of canvass of the parish for financial pledges for the coming year comprise the whole stewardship program. Other congregations may conduct more elaborate efforts, but the focus usually remains on financial needs.

Christian Stewardship *does* involve a responsible management of the financial affairs of a church, as well as those of an individual or family. A stewardship development program *does* encourage financial support from the church membership, but money matters are only one part of the whole stewardship picture. *Christian Stewardship is more than fund-raising.*

Christian Stewardship can be thought of as an attitude. *Webster's Dictionary* defines "attitude" as "posture; position assumed or studied to serve a purpose. . .position or bearing as indicating action, feeling, or mood." It is an attitude that influences our daily life. It is a lifestyle, reflected in the way we live our lives every day of the year.

Our understanding of this stewardship attitude originates in Genesis. The first chapter tells us that God created all things, including people, who are to be the managers, caretakers, or stewards of all that God created. Being good stewards involves protecting and improving our natural surroundings and environment. It includes being concerned about the welfare of our fellow human beings. It even means that we are to take care of ourselves, not in a selfish or materialistic way, but rather by staying in shape spiritually, emotionally, mentally, and physically.

Churches provide resources and guidance for our stewardship efforts. Stewardship of the environment is a subject which is receiving an increasing amount of attention at local and national levels of church leadership. Stewardship of the lives of our fellow human beings has always been reflected in the work of all of the denominations. Stewardship of our own lives has been aided by clergy and laity alike.

Of course we share our concern in these areas with others who have no religious orientation, and many of the reasons for our interest and actions are the same...socioeconomic conditions, crime prevention, and human welfare in general. But we who are Christians have an additional reason; *our concern for the environment, and for the welfare of our fellow human beings, and for our own spiritual and mental and physical condition is part of our faith.*

Understanding Christian Stewardship in a broader and deeper dimension, and seeing the Church as a prime vehicle for its implementation, our personal relationship to the local congregation, as well as to our denomination as a whole, is seen in a new light. Ideally, we are then ready to "throw ourselves into it" in new and stronger ways. We are ready to consider the specifics of Time and Talent and Treasure and a contribution of all three "Ts" as an offering of our very selves to the role of steward of God's Creation.

The issue of motivation, the "why bother?" question, is often overlooked. The role of caretaker or steward is being *offered* to us. We are free to accept or reject the responsibility because of the free will which God has given us. We have a choice to make. We, ourselves, are the ones who decide whether or not to accept the role which God is offering.

A life of Christian Stewardship can be seen as one of the ways in which we offer thanks to God for what God is already doing for us. It be can be our personal response to the sending of His own Son into the world for our sake. It can be a thank-offering given in appreciation for something which has happened in our personal lives.

In summary:
— God is the Creator.
— God has created all things and continues to do so.
— Everthing belongs to God.
— We are offered the role of caretaker, or manager or steward, of God's Creation.
— Taking care of God's Creation includes, at least, concern for
our natural resources and the environment, our fellow human
beings, and ourselves.
— The Church is a primary resource and channel for the
implementation of our personal stewardship.
— Our offerings of time and talents and treasure are really
offerings of our very selves to the role of steward
of God's Creation, through the Church, and beyond.
— Motivation for a life of stewardship derives from our
realization of what God has done and continues to
do for us and our desire to offer our most sincere
thanksgivings for those gifts.

This manual describes a year-round process through which any congregation of any size or description can be assisted in achieving a broader and deeper understanding of the Christian stewardship attitude and the ways in which it can be implemented. It describes 1) an ongoing information process, which is intended to offer a maximum amount of information in regard to the Church's mission and ministry to a maximum number of people throughout the church's entire membership; 2) a long-range planning process, offering an opportunity for development of a greater sense of involvement within the local church membership; 3) a Planning Conference, which draws together all the official leadership of the church to develop a tentative "blueprint" for the next three years; 4) the use of a "Percentage Goal" as a means of directing the attention of the congregation toward a practice of proportionate giving of personal time and talent and treasure with the tithing standard in mind; 5) arrangements for an "Event," usually a dinner or a Sunday brunch for the whole membership, which includes a brief presentation by the Stewardship Committee; 6) a Commitment Sunday; and 7) participation of as many church members as appropriate and possible in each step of the process.

The manual also contains suggestions and materials that are helpful in the recording and monitoring of the year's effort. The appendices contain a plan for a mid-year review program, information in regard to capital or special campaigns, a description of a "space-usage study" procedure for church facilities, an illustration of how Peter Drucker's "management by objective" approach can be used in planning and programming for the local church. An article describing the establishment of a diocesan-wide program in the Canadian Diocese of Niagara follows this introduction.

The 1993 edition of the manual introduced a slightly different vocabulary:

"Commitment" Sunday replaced **"Stewardship" Sunday**—maintaining that Christian Stewardship is really a year-round matter, while at least one Sunday of the year is still designated as an occasion for formal commitments;

Stewardship **"Program"** was used instead of Stewardship **"Campaign,"** the former being more appropriate for a year-round educational effort, while the latter connotes a fund-raising effort;

"Contact Person" took the place of **"Visitor"** or **"Canvasser"** — the latter terms are related to traditional every-member canvasses, wherein each household is visited by one or more persons. However, many congregations are now receiving as many commitment cards as possible after the Commitment Sunday services, and then using "contact persons" to follow up on those who were not present.

Accepting the role which God is offering and becoming a true steward of God's whole Creation is truly a privilege. To fulfill the role, we rely upon faith and prayer and sacrifice. These are the keys to stewardship development in its broadest dimensions. Faith provides motivation. Prayer reinforces faith. Sacrifice reflects faith and prayer and relates both to our daily life.

A Note from Canada

The Rev. Richard M. Jones,
Director of Stewardship and Development for the Diocese of Niagara

This manual is a step-by-step guide for Christian education in stewardship, an issue that includes all the major aspects of our lives—environment, social justice, health, spiritual and financial resources. The methodology outlined here has been tested in the fires of congregational life for nearly thirty years and has been used in congregations of all sizes in urban, suburban, and rural areas. It represents the applied lifetime experience of the author as he has taught stewardship in several countries and in different languages.

I have been using this method of stewardship education in the Anglican Diocese of Niagara, Ontario, Canada, for the past two years. In that time, forty* congregations have started to use this program with positive results. Often when people talk about stewardship, there is a deep desire to apply the theory to everyday personal and congregational life. The great benefit of David Gordon's approach is that it provides a process that meets people where they are and then encourages them to grow in the life of Christian stewardship. This is a manual for congregational leaders who have a responsibility for teaching. It is not a manual of theory but rather a process for education and development that, if conscientiously followed, helps individuals and congregations find a renewed commitment to Christian stewardship in all its dimensions. I commend to you this guidebook to the journey of Christian stewardship and development.

A Regional Approach to Stewardship Education and Development

Introduction

There are a variety of ways to approach the materials in this manual. As any good cook knows, the best results come from following a recipe carefully at the start and then customizing to suit one's taste after really understanding the process. Leaders who conscientiously follow the directions can apply the approach to stewardship education and development outlined in this manual to congregations.

A second approach is to have David Gordon, or a consultant trained by him, guide your congregation through the year. This usually involves four or five visits at critical points in the year's process.

A third approach is the one that was pioneered by David and me in the Anglican diocese of Niagara. In this process the training that could be done together was done at regional meetings of many congregations together. In addition, a group of stewardship consultants has helped a large number of congregations in their Parish Planning Conferences. An outline of this approach, which has helped a large number of congregations begin to use the program with some real assistance from consultants, follows.

The Regional Approach

The Introductory Presentation
In January of the year, congregations are invited to regional meetings to hear about this approach to stewardship education and development. An introduction to the year-round plan is given in a workshop lasting about four hours. All interested congregational leaders are invited, but the Stewardship Committees, Clergy, and Wardens or equivalent decision makers are particularly encouraged to attend. David Gordon or someone trained by him should conduct this workshop.

*Editor's note: The number of congregations is now 62.

First Meeting of the Stewardship Committee
A trained consultant or consultants meet with the congregational stewardship committee. The tasks as outlined in the manual are outlined and the important Stewardship Program Calendar is created.

The Parish Planning Conference (May or June)
The consultants come back to lead this day. A consultant will usually have made at least a telephone contact prior to the event to confirm arrangements.

Regional Meetings for Stewardship Committees, and
Arrangements and Commitment Subcommittees (September)
This is a training event to prepare hosts and hostesses for the "Event" and the team captains of the Commitment subcommittee for their work in recruiting contact people. This training session should include the full quota of people as described in the manual. David or an appropriately trained person should lead this session. It takes about two hours and is conducted on a weekend or weeknight.

Regional Meetings for the Stewardship Committee, Commitment Subcommittee, and
the Contact People (November)
This is session II of "Suggested Briefing Sessions for Contact Persons" as outlined on page 32 of the manual. This session tends to be large as well, and can increase energy and reduce anxiety prior to "Commitment Sunday." Once again it is good to have David or a well-trained person lead this three-hour regional meeting.

Final Stewardship Meeting for the Year
Ideally the consultants who have been working with the congregation would participate in this final meeting to review, evaluate, and plan for the next year.

The Role of the Local Judiciary Stewardship Leaders

This regional approach requires a good volunteer management system that recruits, trains, and deploys people as well as handling evaluation and recognition of everyone's efforts. All of these areas need to be carefully addressed in the process.

- Recruitment must be done with a written job description. A good job description includes role, responsibility, time commitment, training, support offered and benefits to the volunteer and Church.

- Training for consultants can be arranged with David Gordon or someone trained by him. An annual training weekend in February is ideal to prepare consultants for their parish responsibilities. The annual training events will be most valuable if all consultants are invited. The group can become a learning organization if time is given for individuals to share case studies of congregational experience and other resources.

- Deployment must be carefully monitored to ensure an appropriate match between consultants and parishes. This requires knowledge of the strengths and weaknesses of consultants and the special needs of particular congregations. It is recommended that consultants be sent in teams of two to parishes if possible. This provides the team with a higher degree of team-awareness, as one person can always be a process observer while the other is working.

- Evaluation of the consultants can be done through consultant reports of the event and evaluation forms sent to the Parish Stewardship Committees. Personal contact with consultants during the year by the judiciary leaders is also desirable.

- Recognition is often a forgotten element in church organizations. We suggest a form of recognition that could be combined with the training weekend but not necessarily confined to a once-only event. Personal written recognition from the judiciary is also appropriate, as is acknowledgment of this ministry at denominational gatherings.

In Conclusion

The regional approach to stewardship education and development has the advantage of bringing a large number of congregations into the program quickly. It offers those congregations consultant support and the energy that comes from doing something with others. It offers the judiciary an opportunity to develop many trained and committed stewardship consultants. These individuals enrich the life of their own congregations and the congregations they serve in the denomination. Finally, by charging a small one-time fee to participating congregations, it is possible to fund consultant help such as that provided by David Gordon or persons trained by him.

GETTING STARTED EARLY IN THE YEAR is one of the keys to a successful program. Appointment of the Stewardship Committee and the scheduling of an organizational meeting before the end of January allows for a more relaxed schedule for the rest of the year, as well as for a greater awareness of the stewardship program on the part of church membership.

Arranging the Calendar at the beginning of the year will avoid scheduling conflicts. Beginning the Information Process as soon as possible after this initial meeting of the committee will provide a growing appreciation of the church's mission and ministry. Using the full long-range planning time allotment will enhance the results in terms of the number of participants and quality of their responses.

An early start for the stewardship program contrasts directly with the practices of many congregations. Since Stewardship has so often been understood only as a way of funding the budget, local programs have been dollar focused, and activities have consisted of little more than a solicitation of financial pledges during the fall. Aside from the practical benefits of a year-round program, beginning early is also the first step in helping a church recognize that Christian Stewardship is really a matter for concern and attention twenty-four hours of the day, every day of the year. A year-round stewardship effort also helps congregations realize that Stewardship is more than simply raising funds.

Appointment of the Stewardship Committee

* Chosen with careful consideration of the qualifications of its members—creative, enthusiastic, and dedicated persons with leadership abilities; usually appointed by Rector, Vicar, or Wardens;

* The *Chairperson*, appointed to a two-year term for the sake of continuity in programming and as a step toward the development of experienced leadership;

* The *Vice-Chairperson*, an understudy of the Chairperson, serving in this position for two years, then succeeding the Chairperson; may also carry responsibility for the Long-Range Planning Process;

* The *Secretary*, who will keep minutes of the committee's meetings and oversee production and distribution of letters and materials to the parish;

* An *Information Coordinator* serves as the Convener of the Information Subcommittee of the Stewardship Committee, which is responsible for planning and implementing a program which informs the congregation in regard to the work of the Church at all levels;

* An *Arrangements Coordinator* who chairs the Arrangements Subcommittee of the Stewardship Committee, which will plan a parish "Event" (e.g., a dinner or Sunday brunch) and assist in securing the attendance for same.

* A *Commitment Coordinator* who is responsible for the enlistment and training of "Contact Persons" and the supervision of their work with the parish membership;

* Each member of the committee is expected to demonstrate personal commitment to Our Lord, Jesus Christ, through regular prayer, church attendance, and a daily life of stewardship of God's Creation;

* The committee meets as soon as possible after the beginning of the year, and monthly thereafter, and reports regularly to the Vestry or Bishop's Committee.

Stewardship Committee Meetings Begin

* *Materials needed:* Current parish list, parish calendar for the coming year, individual copies of the manual;

* *Agenda items:* 1) determination of regular meeting schedule,
    2) clarification of responsibilities of committee members,
    3) development of the Stewardship Program Calendar (p. 7)
    4) planning for the initiation of the "Information Process" (i.e., selection of subcommittee members, discussion of techniques for communication)(p. 9)
    5) preparation for the Long-Range Planning Process (p. 11)

Stewardship Committee Roster

Year:_____

PARISH: _____

Address: _____

_____

Telephone: _____

Fax: _____ E-mail: _____

Rector/Vicar: _____

CHAIRPERSON:

Full Name: _____

Address: _____

_____

Telephones: (Home)_____ (Office)_____

Fax: _____ E-mail: _____

VICE-CHAIRPERSON:

Full Name: _____

Address: _____

_____

Telephones: (Home)_____ (Office)_____

Fax: _____ E-mail: _____

SECRETARY:

Full Name: _____

Address: _____

_____

Telephones: (Home)_____ (Office)_____

Fax: _____ E-mail: _____

INFORMATION COORDINATOR:

Full Name: _____

Address: _____

_____

Telephones: (Home)_____ (Office)_____

Fax: _____ E-mail: _____

ARRANGEMENTS COORDINATOR:

Full Name: _____

Address: _____

_____

Telephones: (Home)_____ (Office)_____

Fax: _____ E-mail: _____

COMMITMENT COORDINATOR:

Full Name: _____

Address: _____

_____

Telephones: (Home)_____ (Office)_____

Fax: _____ E-mail: _____

THE STEWARDSHIP PROGRAM CALENDAR clarifies the steps to be taken through the year, while helping to avoid scheduling conflicts. The format suggested on the next page of this manual is arranged to show the sequence and approximate time of the year for each part of the program. The exact dates are determined by the local Stewardship Committee. A sample calendar has been included for parishes using *November 8, 1998,* for Commitment Sunday. It illustrates the appropriate intervals to be maintained, whether this date is used or whether the local Commitment Sunday is shifted to earlier or later dates.

Dates in the January through August section are determined by working from top to bottom, lines 1-8. In the September through December schedule, experience has shown that it is easier to work from bottom to top, lines 22-9. The procedure can be done as follows: 1) determine the date of Commitment Sunday; 2) set the date of the parish "Event" (p. 39), usually a week or ten days prior to the Commitment Sunday (p. 42); 3) schedule the clergy letter (p. 41) to arrive in the week following the Event, and the Stewardship Chairperson's and Senior Warden's letters (p. 37-38) at about two-week intervals preceding the clergy letter; 4) schedule the Host/Hostess telephone calls to follow each of the first two letters; 5) schedule the Contact-Person training sessions, Team Captains' reminder calls, "Letter of Invitation" (p. 30) mailing, and telephone confirmation calls; 6) schedule the first meeting of the Arrangements and Commitment Subcommittees (p. 22) prior to the "Letter of Invitation" telephone confirmation calls.

The Stewardship Committee maintains a regular meeting schedule in order to monitor the program through the year. The September meeting is held in conjunction with the first meeting of the Arrangements and Commitment Subcommittees, and the October meeting can coincide with the contact-person training session. July and August meetings are usually not necessary.

A Sample Stewardship Program Calendar

JANUARY–FEBRUARY	1. First meeting of Stewardship Committee	1	_2/1 to 2/8_
	2. Deadline for first meeting of Information Subcommittee	2	_2/22_
	3. Deadline for first meeting of Long-Range Planning Committee	3	_2/22_
MARCH–APRIL	Long-Range Planning Idea-Gathering		
APRIL–MAY–JUNE	4. Parish Planning Conference	4	_May or June_
JULY–AUGUST	5. Deadline for appointment of Arrangements and Commitment Subcommittees	5	_8/31_
	6. Deadline for completion of stewardship brochure, except for final names	6	_8/31_
	7. Deadline for updating of parish list ("Family" and "Individual" units)	7	_8/31_
	8. Deadline for preparation of contact-person information cards, pledge cards, and telephoning assignment cards	8	_8/31_
SEPTEMBER–OCTOBER	9. First meeting of Arrangements and Commitment Subcommittees with Stewardship Committee	9	_9/13 to 9/20_
	10. "Letter of Invitation" to be mailed to prospective contact persons, to be received by...	10	_9/21_
	11. Telephone confirmations of contact persons' acceptances by Commitment Subcommittee, assisted by Stewardship Committee	11	_9/27 to 9/30_
	12. Senior Warden's letter to parish, with stewardship brochure enclosed, mailed—to be received by...	12	_10/5_
	13. Arrangements Subcommittee's first telephone invitation to each household unit for the "Event"	13	_10/11 to 10/14_
	14. Stewardship Chairperson's letter, with proportionate giving worksheet enclosed, mailed—to be received by...	14	_10/19_
	15. Arrangements Subcommittee's second telephone call to each household unit re the "Event"	15	_10/25 to 10/28_
	16. Contact person–reminder calls by Commitment Subcommittee regarding training sessions:	16	_10/4 to 10/7_
	17. 1) contacting instructions,	17	_10/11_
	18. 2) information re local church	18	_10/25_
OCTOBER–NOVEMBER	19. The "Event"	19	_10/29 to 11/1_
	20. Clergy letter mailed to the parish, to be received by...	20	_11/2_
	21. COMMITMENT SUNDAY	21	_11/8_
NOVEMBER–DECEMBER	22. Final Stewardship Committee meeting for year (review, evaluation, planning)	22	_January 1999_

A Stewardship Program Calendar

(Your Dates)

JANUARY–FEBRUARY	1. First meeting of Stewardship Committee	1 _____
	2. Deadline for first meeting of Information Subcommittee	2 _____
	3. Deadline for first meeting of Long-Range Planning Committee	3 _____
MARCH–APRIL	Long-Range Planning Idea-Gathering	
APRIL–MAY–JUNE JULY–AUGUST	4. Parish Planning Conference	4 _____
	5. Deadline for appointment of Arrangements and Commitment Subcommittees	5 _____
	6. Deadline for completion of stewardship brochure, except for final names	6 _____
	7. Deadline for updating of parish list ("Family" and "Individual" units)	7 _____
	8. Deadline for preparation of contact-person information cards, pledge cards, and telephoning assignment cards	8 _____
SEPTEMBER–OCTOBER	9. First meeting of Arrangements and Commitment Subcommittees with Stewardship Committee	9 _____
	10. "Letter of Invitation" to be mailed to prospective contact persons, to be received by...	10 _____
	11. Telephone confirmations of contact persons' acceptances by Commitment Subcommittee, assisted by Stewardship Committee	11 ____ to ____
	12. Senior Warden's letter to parish, with stewardship brochure enclosed, mailed—to be received by...	12 _____
	13. Arrangements Subcommittee's first telephone invitation to each household unit for the "Event"	13 _____
	14. Stewardship Chairperson's letter, with proportionate giving worksheet enclosed, mailed—to be received by...	14 _____
	15. Arrangements Subcommittee's second telephone call to each household unit re the "Event"	15 ____ to ____
	16. Contact person–reminder calls by Commitment Subcommittee regarding training sessions:	16 ____ to ____
	17. 1) contacting instructions,	17 _____
	18. 2) information re local church	18 _____
OCTOBER–NOVEMBER	19. The "Event"	19 ____ to ____
	20. Clergy letter mailed to the parish, to be received by...	20 _____
	21. COMMITMENT SUNDAY	21 _____
NOVEMBER–DECEMBER	22. Final Stewardship Committee meeting for year (review, evaluation, planning)	22 _____

AN INFORMED CONGREGATION IS A RESPONSIVE CONGREGATION. The first basic component of this plan is the "Information Process." The responsibility for it rests with the Information Subcommittee of the Stewardship Committee. The purpose of the process is to communicate as much information as possible to as many people as possible throughout the entire church membership. It is an ongoing process, intended to be continued year after year. It is a steady offering of comparatively small bits of information, since this procedure has been found to be more effective then the occasional massive mailing used by some congregations. The information which is being communicated pertains to the mission and ministry of the church at all levels—regional, national, international, as well as local.

Most churches are already doing an information process to some extent. This plan suggests expansion of the present procedures, while also emphasizing the importance of communication as a stewardship development issue.

Improved and expanded methods of communication enhance the life of any church. If church members are to be motivated toward a greater understanding and implementation of Christian Stewardship, knowledge of the mission and ministries being conducted is essential. Personal offerings of time and talent and treasure are proportionate to the individual's understanding and appreciation of the purposes for which the offerings are made. An informed congregation is going to be a more responsive congregation.

The Information Process

* Managed by the Information Subcommittee of the Stewardship Committee;

* Provides a variety of means through which to achieve a greater awareness and understanding of the mission of the church and its fulfillment in the local congregation, deanery, diocese, province, national church, or worldwide Anglican Communion;

* Utilizes bulletin-board displays, videotapes, posters, and other visual means of presenting information;

* May also include organized tours of institutions or other program centers to provide on-site knowledge;

* Offers other firsthand reports through local speakers or visitors;

* Continues on a year-round schedule, year after year;

* Provides an opportunity for involvement of church members who have expertise or special interest in gathering and communicating knowledge of the life of the church at all levels.

First Meeting of the Information Subcommittee

Membership: Stewardship Committee Information Coordinator, plus other qualified and interested persons

Materials needed: Sunday Service leaflet sample
Parish newsletter sample
Parish organizational chart
A list of parish programs and activities
Parish calendar for the year as of meeting date

Agenda: Discussion, planning, and assignment of individual or group responsibilities re:
1) Sunday leaflet inserts,
2) parish newsletter articles,
3) bulletin (display)-board plans and materials,
4) audiovisual materials and usage schedule,
5) speaker's bureau,
6) parish field trips
7) regular meeting schedule for the committee

Subsequent Meetings of the Information Subcommittee

* Recruiting of additional personnel, as needed;

* Monitoring of Information Process, as a whole.

LONG-RANGE PLANNING IS ALSO GOOD STEWARDSHIP. A planning process is included as a basic component of this plan for three reasons. First, planning is an ingredient in good church administration. It offers a sense of direction for the whole membership. It contains specific goals which reflect the purpose of the congregation's very existence. "Mission Statements" (Matthew 28:19 & 20 for the church) and planning ahead are considered to be important in business and industry. So also for the church, rather than having congregations simply exist from one week until the next without any real vision for the future.

Secondly, long-range planning is a part of good stewardship. When we plan, we use what resources we have to the best advantage. A congregation's offerings of time, talents, and treasure are focused on real needs and used in the most effective ways.

A third reason for including the planning process relates directly to personal stewardship development among the church members. The way in which the data used in the planning is secured offers an opportunity for development of a greater sense of involvement or "ownership" for everyone. Everyone is invited to participate, rather than having the work done by a comparatively small number of people (e.g., only the church's governing board, or a subcommittee thereof).

While most churches already do some sort of effective planning, two mistakes are commonly made. The first is formulating a plan without involving the whole constituency, thus losing the opportunity for developing fuller participation and ownership. A second common error is setting long-term future plans with no provision for revision. These kinds of plans often gather dust on a back shelf until they are forgotten completely.

The procedures described in this manual offer corrections for both mistakes. The entire church membership, from the "old-time" members to newcomers, is invited to participate. Even though many will not have any suggestions within a given year, the invitation to do so will often produce a greater sense of involvement. The second mistake is remedied by repeating the planning process each year. Once a plan, or "blueprint" has been devised, it is reviewed and revised in succeeding years with the addition of each year's idea-gathering results. The result is a changing and expanding plan in the midst of a process that continues to create new interest and wider participation.

The Long-Range Planning Committee

*   Formation requested by the Stewardship Committee as part of the year-round stewardship development program;

*   Appointed by the Vestry or Bishop's Committee, drawing from its own membership and/or the rest of the parish membership, maintaining continuity from year to year;

*   A knowledgeable group, aware of the mission of the Church and capable of recognizing needs and opportunities within the local church and community related to the fulfillment of that mission;

*   Gathers ideas for the congregation's future life and work from as many people and groups within the parish as possible, utilizing questionnaires, parish meetings, "firesides," or any other appropriate means—a maximum number of ideas from a maximum number of people is the goal;

*   Recognizes that every idea is important, because the person who submitted the idea is important;

*   Uses thought-provoking questions to elicit responses by questionnaire or in group discussions;

*   Serves for the duration of the annual planning process, and then disbands, unless assigned additional tasks beyond the stewardship program responsibilities.

The First Meeting of the Long-Range Planning Committee

Membership: Usually three to seven people, chosen from among parish members, plus the Rector and Vice-Chair of the Stewardship Committee as ex-officio members

Materials needed: Copies of the Long-Range Planning Letter (p. 13)

Sample Questionnaire from the manual (p. 14)

A current parish membership list

The parish calendar for the year

Agenda: Discussion, planning, and assignment of individual or group responsibilities for:
1) mailing date for planning letter and questionnaire;
2) schedule for Sunday coffee-hour idea-gathering sessions;
3) requests to parish organizations for discussions of the questionnaire in regular meetings of the respective groups;
4) planning for other discussion opportunities, if indicated;
5) preliminary planning for the Parish Planning Conference (site, meal arrangements, equipment, and materials);
6) regular meeting schedule for the LRP Committee

A Sample Long-Range Planning Letter

(Letterhead)

(Date)

Dear

Two of the most important parts of our year-round program of Stewardship Education and Development are the "Information Process" and the "Long-Range Planning Process." The purpose of the former is to offer as much information as possible to as many people as possible about the mission and ministry of the Church at all levels. You will be hearing more and more, not only in regard to things that are happening in our parish, but also in the life of the Episcopal Church beyond our congregational level. We hope that all of our people will be sharers of information, as well as receivers.

The long-range planning steps are intended to give the whole parish an opportunity to participate in setting goals for the next three years. Every member of the parish is important in the life of the parish. The ideas which you have to offer are as vital to the future of our church's ministry as your presence in the services of worship and in all the other ways in which you participate. Every idea which is submitted will receive careful attention. Later in the year, we shall be having a Parish Planning Conference, where all the leaders of the parish will meet to sort through the ideas and produce a tentative "blueprint" for our next three years. Next year, there will be another opportunity for the submission of more ideas, and this year's planning results will be reviewed and revised.

We are enclosing a brief questionnaire. You are invited to share whatever dreams you may have for our church for the next three years. Written responses may be mailed or brought to the parish office. Please turn them in within the next three or four weeks.

There will be an informal meeting of the congregation after each of the services on Sunday, the __(date)__. This will give us an opportunity to discuss ideas together, and, perhaps, be stimulated to offer additional thoughts.

Also, we are asking each of the parish organizations to devote at least one meeting during the next three months to this topic, and there is the possibility of arranging for neighborhood discussion groups.

Thank you for your participation in this very important part of our parish's planning process for this year.

Faithfully,

_____
Chairperson, Parish Long-Range
Planning Committee

Enclosure

A Question

Note: *This is a time to dream. Creative ideas from the congregation are the lifeblood of the healthy parish. Whether we can achieve all of our goals in the immediate future is not the issue. We want to know the unknown needs and to hear the unheard ideas.*

IF RESOURCES WERE UNLIMITED, WHAT WOULD YOU LIKE TO SEE OUR LOCAL CHURCH DOING OVER THE NEXT THREE YEARS?

14

THE PARISH PLANNING CONFERENCE is a key meeting of the year. It is conducted in the late spring in order that the results may be used during the remaining months of the year. Attended by the Vestry or Bishop's Committee, the Stewardship Committee, the Long-Range Planning Committee, representatives of all organizations within the parish, any other persons in leadership roles, diocesan convention delegates and alternates, and the clergy, it is located, ideally, away from the local church facilities to provide a fresh setting and freedom from distractions. A Saturday meeting, including lunch and/or dinner and a period of relaxation, has worked very well for a number of churches. Alternatively, some parishes have utilized Sunday afternoons, using a similar schedule.

The agenda (p. 18) includes: 1) a presentation in regard to the nature and function of the Church in order to gain a perspective for the rest of the day's work; 2) a review, evaluation, and priority-setting of the ideas gathered during the preceding months, together with additional ideas evolving from among the conference participants; 3) an estimation of the dollar amounts needed to meet the new goals for the coming year, as well as to continue existing programs and activities; 4) the conversion of the "Dollar Goal" to a "Minimum Percentage Goal" for the forthcoming commitment program.

The Parish Planning Conference, which is really a "think tank," does not produce a parish budget for the coming year. This is done by the Vestry or Bishop's Committee, after the Commitment Sunday, when the work can be done in a realistic and final way.

The conference completes the planning process for the year. As soon as possible, the conference results are shared with the congregation through meetings and/or mailings. The "blueprint" for the next three years will reflect the congregation's participation in the process, give a new sense of "ownership" in the life of the parish, and lay a sound foundation for future stewardship.

The Minimum Percentage Goal is announced as part of the conference report and further publicized in the ensuing months through newsletters, bulletins, posters, announcements, and other ways.

A Sample Invitation for Parish Leaders

(Date)

MEMO

TO: THE VESTRY, THE STEWARDSHIP COMMITTEE, THE LONG-RANGE PLANNING COMMITTEE, ORGANIZATION AND PROGRAM LEADERS, REPRESENTATIVES TO EXTRA-PAROCHIAL PROGRAMS OR ORGANIZATIONS

FROM: (Name), CHAIR, PARISH PLANNING CONFERENCE
(Date, place, time)

SUBJECT: PLANNING CONFERENCE INFORMATION

As you know, our parish is involved in a Long-Range Planning Process as part of our stewardship program. The entire membership of our church has been invited to participate by offering ideas for our ministry during the next three years. We have circulated a questionnaire and offered a variety of opportunities for group discussions.

The next step is for the leadership of the parish to meet in a Parish Planning Conference, at which time we shall do four things:

1) Spend some time talking about the Church — who we are, why we are here;

2) Hear all of the ideas which have been submitted to the Long-Range Planning Committee through questionnaires or discussions, and add any others which come to mind;

3) Develop a tentative "blueprint" for the next three years, based on the data on hand, and establish a "Dollar Goal";

4) Convert our "Dollar Goal" to a "Percentage Goal".

This will be one of the most important meetings of the year for our church. Please make every effort to be present or, if you cannot be with us, to send a representative.

R.S.V.P., (telephone number)

The Parish Planning Conference

Attendance: Parish clergy, all laity who are in leadership roles in the parish, parish representatives to diocesan structural levels beyond the parish, and Diocesan Convention delegate(s) and alternate(s)

Materials needed: Easel

Newsprint and markers

Individual copies of printed compilation of ideas offered by the parish membership (clerical and lay). (Please note: Every idea submitted is represented in the compilation, listed by title; no indication of number of persons or groups submitting the same idea(s); ideas clustered under general headings [i.e., "Parish Education," "Buildings and Groups," "Outreach," et al].)

Arrangements: Ordinarily, the Parish Planning Conference is held away from the home parish (i.e., a neighboring parish hall, a conference center, a parishioner's residence, a school, etc.), stressing the importance and uniqueness of the gathering, as contrasted with routine parish meetings, and also eliminating or reducing less than full attendance;

Approximately four hours of working time is usually needed for completion of the agenda (a Saturday schedule, 10:00 a.m. to 4:00 p.m., including a lunch break and some free time, or a Sunday afternoon from 1:00 to 5:00 p.m., preceded by a luncheon, are common provisions);

Informal dress and relaxed day describe the desired tone of the conference

Agenda: Suggested as follows (parish clergy may be asked to conduct the presentation or discussion in Section I; the Long-Range Planning Committee can be responsible for Sections II, III and IV)

A Sample Agenda for a Planning Conference

Section I.   Perspective. An understanding of the Church.
    A. Introduction—Opening prayer, introduction of stewardship committee by the Rector or Vicar, and a general description of the year-round program by the Chairperson of the Stewardship Committee.
    B. A brief review of the theology of the Church by the Rector or Vicar.

Section II.   Presentation of long-range planning ideas by the Chairperson of the Long-Range Planning Committee.
    A. Every idea submitted by the church membership is included, and conference attendees are welcome to add more in the course of the meeting.
    B. Ideas are presented by "title," omitting the member's reasons for submitting the idea(s).
    C. There is no indication of the popularity of a given idea, even though more than one person may have mentioned it.
    D. Ideas are grouped into appropriate categories in order to facilitate their review. The conference members can be divided into groups with each group being given one or more categories.

Section III.   Preparation of the tentative "Blueprint for Tomorrow" ("tentative" since the assembled group has no authority to make any action decisions, and also because the planning process is repeated each year, and the previous year's "blueprint" is always subject to revision as part of the process).
    A. A chart consisting of six columns is prepared. The first four columns are headed by the present year and the next three years. The other two columns are entitled "Underway" and "Referred."
    B. The ideas are discussed and listed in one of the columns. (The "Referred" column is used for ideas for which more information is needed and for ideas which are not appropriate for inclusion in an actual plan; i.e., suggestions, criticisms, "editorial comments.")
    C. After all of the ideas are on a single chart, cost estimates for those ideas listed for the next calendar year are determined by the conference members.
    D. The estimated cost of new ideas for the coming calendar year, the pledge income amount from the current year's budget, the amount of deficit in the current budget, if any, and an estimate of the net increase, excluding the aforementioned deficit, which would be required in addition to the present year's budget—if it were to be "business as usual" in the coming year—are totaled to produce a "Dollar Goal" for the forthcoming commitment period. It does not represent the entire church budget. Rather, it is an amount which would be represented on the "Pledge Income" line, and would provide for a balanced budget.

Section IV.   The "Dollar Goal" is converted to a "Percentage Goal," using the worksheet on p. 20. The "Percentage Goal" is the minimum percent of household income which church members will be asked to consider as a basis for their pledge.

Planning Conference Worksheet (Optional)

Category:_____   Year of Conference: _____

Item	This Year	Year One	Year One Cost Estimate	Year Two	Year Three	Underway	Referred

Notes: If an idea is general, make a specific proposal to advance the general concept. For instance, if the idea is to do something about illiteracy, you might propose to have an adult reading program. Only ideas for the next year (Year One) are given a cost estimate.

Form courtesy of Rev. Richard D. Sloan, New York, NY

Setting the Minimum Percentage Goal for the Next Year

I.   Review of the present year's giving pattern:

           A. Average annual pledge, this year $_____

           B. Median income estimate for last year $_____

           C. Percent of income pledged (A/B)   _____%

           D. Total number of units in the church   _____

           E. Total number of units pledging this year   _____

           F. Percent of units pledging this year (E/D)   _____%

II.   Determination of the Percentage Goal for the next year:

           A. Number of units expected to pledge for the next year   _____

           B. Median income estimate established by conference
               participants for this year $_____

           C. Total income anticipated within units expected to
               pledge (A x B) $_____

           D. The "Dollar Goal" estimate prepared by conference
               participants for the next year $_____

           E. Average percent of income needed to produce the
               "Dollar Goal" (D/C)   _____%

           F. Minimum Percentage Goal for the next year as determined
               by the conference participants   _____%

NOTE: *Resources for determining median income figures may include information from the local Chamber of Commerce, the U.S. Census, or the Diocesan Stewardship Office. Anonymous averaging of incomes among the participants at the conference, or at least 10 percent of the congregation, will often reflect the average of the parish. Whatever amount is used in the calculations is determined by the conference participants.*

THE SUMMER MONTHS allow time for appointment of the Commitment and Arrangements Subcommittees (p. 22), clerical work (p. 23–24) and preparation of a "local brochure" (p. 27–28).

Even though the two subcommittees will not meet until September, selecting the membership by mid-June is essential. These two committees require very specific time commitments on particular dates. Consequently, recruiting needs to be completed before prospective committee members have filled their fall calendars.

Ideally, members of both committees will be selected carefully with serious attention being paid to their sense of responsibility and leadership capabilities. The subcommittee coordinator, assisted by the other members of the Stewardship Committee, is responsible for the appointments. No one should be asked to serve on both committees. The volume of work would be excessive, and it is important, also, to involve as many people as possible in the operation of the program.

Recruiting conversations should include 1) the importance of the role which is to be performed; 2) a review of the job description; and 3) a definite decision on the part of the prospect to accept the responsibility.

Summer office work includes an updating of the church membership list and preparation of information cards, commitment cards, and a telephoning-assignment procedure, for the Arrangements and Commitment Subcommitees, all based on the membership list. The membership list should be as accurate as possible, including inactive as well as active households or individuals, disregarding whether or not they are currenlty among those who have made formal commitments of their time, talents, or treasure.

The information cards are for the purpose of providing a profile of the household and identifying residents who belong to the church. Telephoning assignments can be handled with sets of 3 x 5 cards or sections of membership lists, although the former facilitates any trading of names. Whichever procedure is followed, separate sets are needed for the Arrangements and Commitment Committees. Reporting forms are illustrated in the manual.

Commitment cards, at least one for every household (family or individual), are also prepared during the summer months, even though they will not be used until Commitment Sunday. Experience has indicated the importance of maintaining a tight control of the cards. Preferably, they are never mailed or given to church members to be returned at a later date. Such practices have been shown to create two major problems. The first is the possibility of a "casual" response, ranging from making commitments without any serious consideration of the matter to mislaying or ignoring the card. This leads to the second problem of not being able to complete the year's program. If there is procrastination, cards which are in the hands of the congregation are difficult to retrieve, and those who are finishing all of the contacts are expected to make only two attempts.

A suggested format for the Local Brochure, which is mailed to the congregation in the fall, is illustrated in the manual.

Appointment of the Commitment Subcommittee

* Responsible for the recruitment and training of contact persons;

* Comprised of the Coordinator and Team Captains *(one captain for each twenty-five house-holds)*;

* Appointed by June 15 to serve until the conclusion of the fall program schedule;

* Expected to meet early in September, receive instructions, and telephone prospective Contact Persons (after they have received the "Letter of Invitation," p. 30) to confirm that they will serve;

* Also expected to call the "confirmed lists" before the briefing sessions, reminding them of the required training and the Commitment Sunday schedule;

* The plan of the committee is to have every family or individual household within the congregation contacted;

* The "Letter of Invitation" is sent to all church members from high-school age and beyond, except for those eliminated by clergy for pastoral reasons (aged, sick, etc.) The larger the number of persons involved in the actual contacting and the preceding preparations, the more successful the program will be.

Appointment of the Arrangements Subcommittee

* Responsible for planning and hosting a parish "Event."

* Comprised of a Coordinator and Hosts and/or Hostesses *(one Host or Hostess for each ten households)*;

* Appointed by June 15 to serve until the conclusion of the fall program;

* Expected to meet early in September, receive instructions, plan the "Event," receive telephoning assignments, and contact parishioners as scheduled.

Preparation of Contact-Person Information Cards

*   The set of Information Cards corresponds to the current parish membership list (families and individuals not included in families);

*   Indicate church affiliation for each member of the household (i.e., Episcopal, Methodist, Roman Catholic, et al., or "none");

*   Consider all information to be confidential and only for office and committee use;

*   "Pledge" column may indicate present pledge amount, if any, or "yes" or "no";

*   Prepare a card for every membership unit, whether or not they are to be visited or contacted by telephone, or will be making a pledge at church;

*   Important pastoral information received in the course of the contact should be recorded on the back of the card for pastoral or office use;

*   Cards are left in alphabetical order, matching the parish membership list, until individual contact assignments are made, either before Commitment Sunday (if the entire parish is to be visited), or after the pledging period at the church on Commitment Sunday;

*   Information Cards are prepared in order that the contact person will have at least a partial profile of the household for which he or she is responsible.

INFORMATION CARD

Name:_____   Tel. _____

Street:_____

City:_____   Zip:_____

Names	Church Affiliation	Active	Inactive	Pledge
_____	_____	_____	_____	_____
_____	_____	_____	_____	_____
_____	_____	_____	_____	_____
_____	_____	_____	_____	_____
_____	_____	_____	_____	_____

Preparation of Commitment Cards

* The set of Commitment Cards corresponds to the current parish membership list and the set of Information Cards;

* The Information Card and the Commitment Card for each household are paired (each including name, address, etc.);

* If pledging is to take place following services on Commitment Sunday, cards are left in alphabetical order; if the parish Stewardship Committee plans to conduct a parish-wide visitation, the cards are prepared prior to assignment to contact persons at their final meeting on Commitment Sunday.

Name:_____ Tel:_____ Street Address:_____ City:_____ Zip:_____	**A STEWARDSHIP COMMITMENT FOR OUR PARISH MINISTRY**

With gratitude to God and as an expression of my personal commitment to Jesus Christ and His Church, it is my intention to offer:

1) the equivalent of _____ hours per week for the Lord's work,

2) using my personal talents for _____

   _____ ;

3) and financial support of $_____ payable at a rate of $_____ per

   _____ week, _____ month, or _____ year.

Signed:_____ Date:_____

Preparation of Reporting Forms for Arrangements and Commitment Subcommittees

* Members of the two groups (Hosts, Hostesses, Team Captains) will receive telephoning assignments at their initial meeting in early September — Hosts and Hostesses (Arrangements Committee) being given all the households of the parish, Team Captains (Commitment Committee) being given the names of those parishioners who are receiving the "Letter of Invitation";

* Reports of the first telephone contacts are reported to the respective Coordinators on the following forms, and the forms are returned to the telephoners for the subsequent calls and reports.

PROSPECTIVE CONTACT-PERSON LIST & REPORT FORM

Team Captain_____

Name:_____ Tel:_____	1st Call		2nd Call	
	yes	no	yes	no
1)_____				
2)_____				
3)_____				
4)_____				
5)_____				
6)_____				
7)_____				
8)_____				
9)_____				
10)_____				

HOST/HOSTESS REPORT FORM

Host/Hostess_____

Name:_____ Tel:_____	1st Call		2nd Call	
	yes	no	yes	no
1)_____				
2)_____				
3)_____				
4)_____				
5)_____				
6)_____				
7)_____				
8)_____				
9)_____				
10)_____				

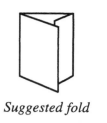

Suggested fold

PLEASE DON'T FORGET!!!!

COMMITMENT SUNDAY

(date)

Services

_____

_____

_____

✝ ✝ ✝

FAITH + PRAYER + SACRIFICE

✝ ✝ ✝

STEWARDSHIP DEVELOPMENT
GROUP

The Stewardship Committee:

Chairperson
Vice-Chairperson
Secretary
Information Coordinator
Arrangements Coordinator
Commitment Coordinator

The Information Subcommittee:

(Names)

The Arrangements Subcommittee:

(Names)

The Commitment Subcommittee:

(Names)

Church Photo

or

Logo

Church name

and

address

Staff

27

SOME THINGS WE ARE DOING . . . .

* A shelter for the homeless—using personnel and financial resources of our congregation in response to a major crisis within our community

* Teen-Town Drop-in Center—a ministry offered to all the youth of the community, providing a creative environment for personal development

* The Telephone Network—daily contact in a specified period for anyone who requests this service

* "Introduction to the New 1982 Hymnal"—an in-depth discussion covering reasons for the changes and additions, and an opportunity to practice hymns and service music

* A new schedule of Daily Morning and Evening Prayer—conducted by our lay readers

* "Thursday for Seniors"—a program of meal and activities for the retired.

* The Office Volunteers, who assist in a multitude of ways in the routine administrative work of the Parish.

SOME THINGS WE HOPE TO ADD . . . .

* A full-time Director of Education to help plan and develop an expansion of our present program

* Major repairs of all of the roofs

* Partial subsidies for sabbaticals and continuing education programs for lay and clergy staff

* Programs and activities for a new singles and/or married group

* Feasibility studies re: retirees' housing, a Parish Day School, and a Lay Ministry Development placement on the parish staff

* Increased financial support to be available for our extra-parochial mission

* Much-needed maintenance for church organ

. . . . REFLECTING SOME OF THE IDEAS SUBMITTED BY THE CONGREGATION DURING OUR PLANNING PROCESS

HOW WE CAN DO IT . . . .

* Our Parish Planning Conference provided an opportunity for an important review of the ministry and mission of our congregation, as we talked about the meaning of the church

* Ideas contributed by many members of our church were reported, considered, and given priorities, and the parish has in hand the tentative "Blueprint" for the next three years

* The Conference established our Minimum Percentage Goal of _____ %, while asking that everyone consider increasing his or her present percentage by at least one additional percentage point

* Proportionate-Giving Worksheets are provided to assist members of the church in their consideration of a financial commitment for the coming year

Step I: We calculate our present percentage level of financial support;

Step II: We consider increasing this percentage by at least 1 percent, or more.

Step III: If this does not bring us to the Minimum Percentage Goal, or beyond, we consider it, also.

28

FALL ACTIVITIES are focused on the recruiting and training of "Contact Persons," the arrangements and the securing of attendance for the "Event," and Commitment Sunday with the Contact Persons' follow-up work. The Commitment Subcommittee of the Stewardship Committee is responsible for the securing and training of the Contact Persons. The Arrangements Sub-committee handles the "Event," except for the program, which is the responsibility of the Stewardship Committee. Commitment Sunday activities are also the responsibility of the Stewardship Committee and the Commitment Subcommittee.

In order to recruit the Contact Persons, a "Letter of Invitation" (p. 30) is mailed to everyone in the parish, including senior-high-age members. (The clergy may wish to withhold some names for pastoral or other reasons, but the list is kept as large as possible). The letter reminds recipients that a stewardship program is underway and also says that they are now being asked to assist in the effort in a very important role. They will be having conversations about Christian Stewardship with other church members. The letter lists the fall schedule of activities related to the stewardship program, including the dates of two training sessions. After receiving the letter, prospects are contacted by members of the Commitment Subcommittee or the Stewardship Committee for confirmation of their acceptance of the invitation. Those persons who are willing to help are recruited into a pool of workers, trained, and then organized into teams led by the Team Captains. Ideally, a Team Captain will be working with three pairs of Contact Persons, and each pair will be responsible for six contacts (or households). Contacts are made in accordance with either "Plan A" or "Plan B" of Commitment Sunday (p. 42).

The involvement of the Hosts and Hostesses of the Arrangements Subcommittee in the work leading up to the "Event" is as important as the "Event" itself. Not only is their awareness of the stewardship program, as a whole, enhanced, but they are involved in a very important way. They will be doing the detail work for the occasion, and they will also be helping to secure the attendance. Along the way, their own understanding of Christian Stewardship will be expanded in the course of a briefing session, as well as in their conversations with fellow church members.

Full membership in the Arrangements and Commitment groups is important. Not only is it felt that the prescribed numbers are important in order to do the work without overburdening smaller organizations, it seems evident, also, that the overall results of the entire year-round effort are proportional to the number of persons involved in each part of the program.

A Sample Letter of Invitation

(Letterhead)

Dear

As you know, our parish is engaged in a year-round program of Stewardship Education and Development. Since early in the year, we have been receiving information in regard to the ministry of our local congregation, the deanery, the diocese, and the Church beyond our borders. During the spring all of us had an opportunity to help set the course for our parish for the next three years. Now we are nearing the time when we shall be invited to make our personal commitment to Our Lord's work. Our response will be a major factor in determining the effectiveness of _____Church.

In order to make a good presentation of our present opportunities, we are calling together a group of our members to contact fellow parishioners. There will be briefing sessions for all workers in order that everyone will have current information as to what our own parish and the Church-at-large are doing. There will also be thorough instruction as to how to do the contacting.

This letter is to serve as our invitation for you to be among those who will be serving our church in this capacity. Within a week one of our Team Captains will call to receive your response to this invitation. Your "yes" will be an important vote for the church.

Thank you for your attention to this matter.

Sincerely yours,

_____
Coordinator, Commitment Subcommittee
___(year)___ Stewardship Program

P.S.

The Briefing Sessions are set for: _____and

_____

Commitment Sunday is: _____

Suggestions for Team Captains' Contacts

* The effectiveness of the forthcoming contacts with the whole parish is in direct proportion to the number of Contact Persons who are recruited and trained to fulfill this responsibility;

* The persons whom you will be contacting will have received a "Letter of Invitation" — you are confirming their acceptance of the invitation;

* The briefings are among the most crucial parts of the stewardship program, and all sessions are important, since they deal with different matters ... and briefings provide self-assurance;

* You are asked to make an initial call to all prospects, recruiting for the "pool," and a second call is made to those who have accepted the invitation, reminding them of the briefing sessions;

* When you call: *Be friendly, regardless of the response*

    Radiate enthusiasm for your church

    Thank your prospects for their willingness to serve

    Report the results to the Coordinator after each series of contacts

* The person whom you are contacting will not necessarily be assigned to your own Contact Team, since team assignments cannot be made until after the briefing sessions;

* All workers will be expected to make their own commitments before contacting other members of the parish.

THOROUGH TRAINING OF CONTACT PERSONS IS EXTREMELY IMPORTANT. Even though some members of the church may have assisted with similar programs in former years, the training is still needed. Many of the methods and materials used in this program are different. Up-to-date information in regard to current conditions or concerns related to the parish, or other levels of church structure, is as important as the latest suggestions as to how to make individual contacts.

Combining the two training sessions into one meeting has not proved to be satisfactory. The amount of material to be covered is excessive, and the individual subjects are of a totally different nature. Consequently, the content of a single gathering is too much to absorb.

Churches sometimes offer a "make-up" session or two, but they are not announced as part of the original schedule. Every effort is made to draw the potential workers to the regular sessions in order to avoid extra work for program leaders. The larger groups are also "morale builders."

Suggested Briefing Sessions for Contact Persons

Session I. The purpose is to acquaint all workers with the life and work of their church and at all levels.
(or II)   A. Opening prayers and/or readings
            B. Review of local church program
                1. "Outreach ministries"
                2. "Inreach ministries"
            C. Highlights of deanery, diocesan, provincial, or national church life which pertain to the local church
            D. Question-and-answer period
            E. Closing prayers and adjournment

Session II. The purpose is to acquaint the visitors with methods for making contacts with parishioners.
(or I)   A. Opening prayers and/or readings
            B. Review of year-round stewardship program
            C. Presentation of contacting techniques
            D. Description of materials
                1. Household Information Cards
                2. Commitment Cards
                3. Other materials which the parish committee may wish to include
            E. Presentation of schedule for Commitment Sunday
            F. Closing prayers and adjournment

* * * * *

PROPORTIONATE-GIVING WORKSHEETS have been found to be very helpful in assisting parishioners as they rethink the matters of proportionate giving and tithing.

Four steps are involved: 1) each individual or family calculates the current proportionate-giving level; 2) an increase of 1 percent, or more, is added to the present level; 3) the total percentage is raised to the parish's minimum percentage goal, if it has not met or exceeded it; 4) the final percentage is applied to expected income to arrive at a dollar amount for the new commitment.

The worksheets are included with the Stewardship Chairperson's letter (with explanation). They can also be distributed at the "Event," or after church services, or in a special mailing. The goal is to have the worksheets in everyone's hands a week or ten days prior to the time when they will be making a personal commitment. The time interval provides opportunity for serious thought in regard to the matter.

Proportionate-Giving Worksheet

"Proportionate giving" means that shares of our personal resources of time and talents and treasure are being devoted to the Lord's work on a regular schedule. It is a commitment made in response to the love which God has shown for us through His Son, Jesus Christ, as well as in events of daily life. It is an offering of "ourselves, our souls and bodies."

Tithing is a standard by which we measure our offerings. All that we are and all that we have has come from God and still belongs to God and is to be used for God's glory. Within that context the biblical tithe (10 percent) becomes a minimum goal in deciding what portion of our resources will be given.

This worksheet offers a means of determining one's present percentage level of pledged financial support for the local church and establishing a commitment for the coming year. It is not to be returned to the church. It is intended for personal use with prayerful consideration in the privacy of your home.

I.   To find your current level of local church support, divide your annual pledge by your income for the same period.

		Example:	Your figures:
A.	Current income	$ 20,000	$_____
B.	Current pledge	$ 600	$_____
C.	Current percentage level (Divide line B by line A)	3%	____%

II. A financial commitment for the coming year might be based on one of the following options:

    A. Tithing

		Example:	Your figures:
1.	Expected income	$ 21,000	$_____
2.	The tithe	10%	10%
3.	New commitment (Multiply line 1 by line 2)	$ 2,100	$_____

    B. Increasing the present level by at least 1 percent.

1.	Expected income	$ 21,000	$_____
2.	Current percentage plus 1%	4%	____%
3.	New commitment	$ 840	$_____

    C. Adopting the church goal

1.	Expected income	$ 21,000	$_____
2.	Minimum percentage goal	5%	____%
3.	New commitment	$ 1050	$_____

Revised form courtesy of John D. Gordon, Christ Church, Seattle, WA

This chart is offered as additional assistance as you determine your financial commitment for the year. The various percentages of annual income are expressed in annual amounts, which are then remitted in weekly, monthly, quarterly, semi-annual, or annual offerings.

ANNUAL INCOME	ANNUAL PERCENTAGES OF INCOME AND DOLLAR AMOUNTS									
	1%	2%	3%	4%	5%	6%	7%	8%	9%	10%
100,000	1,000	2,000	3,000	4,000	5,000	6,000	7,000	8,000	9,000	10,000
97,500	975	1,950	2,925	3,900	4,875	5,850	6,825	7,800	8,775	9,750
95,000	950	1,900	2,850	3,800	4,750	5,700	6,650	7,600	8,550	9,500
92,500	925	1,850	2,775	3,700	4,625	5,550	6,475	7,400	8,325	9,250
90,000	900	1,800	2,700	3,600	4,500	5,400	6,300	7,200	8,100	9,000
87,500	875	1,750	2,625	3,500	4,375	5,250	6,125	7,000	7,875	8,750
85,000	850	1,700	2,550	3,400	4,250	5,100	5,950	6,000	7,650	8,500
82,500	825	1,650	2,475	3,300	4,125	4,950	5,775	6,600	7,425	8,250
80,000	800	1,600	2,400	3,200	4,000	4,800	5,600	6,400	7,200	8,000
77,500	775	1,550	2,325	3,100	3,875	4,650	5,425	6,200	6,975	7,750
75,000	750	1,500	2,250	3,000	3,750	4,500	5,250	6,000	6,750	7,500
72,500	725	1,450	2,175	2,900	3,625	4,350	5,075	5,800	6,525	7,250
70,000	700	1,400	2,100	2,800	3,500	4,200	4,900	5,600	6,300	7,000
67,500	675	1,350	2,025	2,700	3,375	4,050	4,725	5,400	6,075	6,750
65,000	650	1,300	1,950	2,600	3,250	3,900	4,550	5,200	5,850	6,500
62,500	625	1,250	1,875	2,500	3,125	3,750	4,375	5,000	5,625	6,250
60,000	600	1,200	1,800	2,400	3,000	3,600	4,200	4,800	5,400	6,000
57,500	575	1,150	1,725	2,300	2,875	3,450	4,025	4,600	5,175	5,750
55,000	550	1,100	1,650	2,200	2,750	3,300	3,850	4,400	4,950	5,500
52,500	525	1,050	1,575	2,100	2,625	3,150	3,675	4,200	4,725	5,250
50,000	500	1,000	1,500	2,000	2,500	3,000	3,500	4,000	4,500	5,000
47,500	475	950	1,425	1,900	2,375	2,850	3,325	3,800	4,275	4,750
45,000	450	900	1,350	1,800	2,250	2,700	3,150	3,600	4,050	4,500
42,500	425	850	1,275	1,700	2,125	2,550	2,975	3,400	3,825	4,250
40,000	400	800	1,200	1,600	2,000	2,400	2,800	3,200	3,600	4,000
37,500	375	750	1,125	1,500	1,875	2,250	2,625	3,000	3,375	3,750
35,000	350	700	1,050	1,400	1,750	2,100	2,450	2,800	3,150	3,500
32,500	325	650	975	1,300	1,625	1,950	2,275	2,600	2,925	3,250
30,000	300	600	900	1,200	1,500	1,800	2,100	2,400	2,700	3,000
27,500	275	550	825	1,100	1,375	1,650	1,925	2,200	2,475	2,750
25,000	250	500	750	1,000	1,250	1,500	1,750	2,000	2,250	2,500
22,500	225	450	675	900	1,125	1,350	1,575	1,800	2,025	2,250
20,000	200	400	600	800	1,000	1,200	1,400	1,600	1,800	2,000
17,500	175	350	525	700	875	1,050	1,225	1,400	1,575	1,750
15,000	150	300	450	600	750	900	1,050	1,200	1,350	1,500
12,500	125	250	375	500	625	750	875	1,000	1,125	1,250
10,000	100	200	300	400	500	600	700	800	900	1,000
7,500	75	150	225	300	375	450	525	600	675	750
5,000	50	100	150	200	250	300	350	400	450	500
2,500	25	50	75	100	125	150	175	200	225	250

PROPORTIONATE GIVING OF TIME AND TALENTS is as important as our regular offerings of treasure. Church members can be encouraged to make this kind of contribution as well. One way to consider the matter seriously is to look at the number of hours in the day, see that two-thirds of the day is probably devoted to work and rest, and that eight hours of "net time" still remain. That amounts to 480 minutes, and a tithe of that time is forty-eight minutes. The figure is rounded off to an hour, and it is suggested that the congregation offer the equivalent of an hour per day for the Lord's work. Some people may wish to use the "gross" figure of a full twenty-four hours of the day and offer three hours.

A serious consideration of talent offerings can begin with church members making private list of things that they are "really good at." These are their talents, their "gifts from God." One may be a great cook. Another may have special abilities in business affairs. Others may be able to paint or wire a house. Everyone has talents of one kind or another.

Time and talents are always intertwined in daily life, so members select which talents they are going to exercise, and for how much time, and the offering is made.

Four steps are involved in making contributions of time, talent, and treasure. First, we look at what we have. Second, we decide to set aside a portion of our resources specifically for the Lord's work (proportionate giving). Third, we set a standard for ourselves, always having the tithe in mind. Fourth, we decide where to give our offerings. The first three steps are stewardship-development steps. The fourth is the time-, talent-, or treasure-raising step. The first three steps are related, directly, to our understanding of Christian Stewardship and why we give at all. The fourth step determines the targets for our giving.

The same four steps help to show the difference between "fund-raising" and Christian stewardship development. The difference is in where we begin. In the fund-raising approach, we focus first on needs. The church may need a new building, or there may be some other special project for which offerings are to be asked. Capital campaigns, or other special appeals, fall into this category. On the other hand, stewardship development focuses first on what we have and our desire to use our resources as stewards of God's Creation.

It seems evident that difficulties experienced by some congregations in their stewardship development programs may be the result of starting at the fourth step with their appeals, asking members to give to this or that without providing a foundation of stewardship education, nor thinking through the first three steps shown above.

OTHER LETTERS AND TELEPHONE CALLS serve a double purpose. They provide information and serve as additional reminders of the stewardship program.

The Senior Warden's letter is followed by the first telephone invitations for the parish "Event," and the Stewardship Chairperson's letter is followed by a second call to each household, confirming the "YESs," securing a decision from the "MAYBEs," and, ideally, offering a second chance to receive a positive response from the "NOs."

Results of calls should be reported, together with any information received for the office or the clergy.

The calls offer an excellent opportunity to build new relationships and to exercise a lay ministry. Invitations should be personalized to the greatest extent possible, offering to greet the potential guests at the door, having them sit at the Host or Hostess's table, and securing transportation where needed.

A Sample Senior Warden's Letter

(Letterhead)

(Date)

Dear friends,

Commitment Sunday is set for _____ Parish on _____(date)_____ . This will be an important day for all of us. Many of our people have been working long and hard to make it a success. This letter is intended to express my personal thanks and the appreciation of the Vestry for the time and energy which has been expended.

This is also my opportunity to invite your participation during the coming weeks, as we bring this year's stewardship program to its completion. Specifically, I have two requests: first, that you plan to be with us for the ____("Event")___ on _____ , and, secondly, that you be at one of the services on Commitment Sunday _____.

I am convinced that we have among us the capability of fulfilling our mission in this place. I believe that our church deserves our support, and I hope that you feel the same way. During the past months, our Stewardship Committee has attempted to help us all become as fully informed as possible about the church's ministry at all levels. Now we are about to make our response.

Our ____("Event")___ will give all of us an occasion to be together in Christ's fellowship, to hear some exciting things about our parish, and to become informed in regard to the plans for our Commitment Sunday.

I hope that you will read the enclosed brochure and then share it with someone else who may be interested in the work of our parish. It tells some exciting things from the past year and lists our major opportunities for the coming year, reflecting results from our long-range planning process of last spring. It also indicates how we can do the things we would like to do.

Thank you again for your continued interest and support.

Sincerely yours,

_____

Senior Warden

A Sample Stewardship Chairperson's Letter

(Letterhead)

(Date)

To the parish,

You are probably already aware of our Percentage Goal for this year's canvass. This represents our best "guesstimate" of the percentage of household income in our parish which is a reasonable minimum target for the coming year. We are hopeful that all pledges will reflect at least this amount, while all contributors are urged to increase their present level by at least 1 percent or more. The higher percentages which many of us are already contributing help to balance the lower percentages which are necessary for others.

The Episcopal Church has resolved that the biblical tithe of 10 percent be the minimum standard for our financial stewardship. Our parish uses a Percentage Goal rather than a Dollar Goal in order to help us consider the tithe, and to move toward that level of giving and surpass it, as many already have done. We, of course, do not know the actual income within the parish, but we do believe that a practice of proportionate giving by all of our people, moving toward and beyond the tithe as quickly as possible, will provide the financial support for the ministry within our parish, community, and world that surround us.

I am pleased that you and I share a part of our lives within this Christian fellowship, and I look forward to seeing you at the ___("Event")___ on____(date)____.

Faithfully,

_____
Chairman, Stewardship Committee

P.S. The enclosed "Proportionate-Giving Worksheet" is intended to be of assistance in calculating your financial commitment for the coming year.

"The Event" *(Parish dinner, breakfast, brunch, lunch, or whatever)*

* An important part of the preparation for the Commitment Sunday.

* Sometimes served free of charge; sometimes a "planned potluck"; sometimes done on an exchange basis with a neighboring parish—the Arrangements Committee of the home parish plans and prepares the food and decorates, and the neighboring parish serves and cleans up.

* Ordinarily, 50 to 75 percent of the congregation will attend the "Event." It may be necessary to move it to facilities outside the local church.

* Attendance is secured through the work of the Arrangements Committee Hostesses' telephone contacts, as well as with the help of routine parish mailings, etc.

* The program is the responsibility of the Stewardship Committee.

* Provision should be made for the younger children at a separate location, if possible; junior and senior high school students can usually benefit by attending as part of their preparation for participation in the program.

Suggestions for Hostesses and Hosts

* Please telephone or personally contact each household on your list to extend an invitation to the parish "Event."

* Urge attendance of all adults and senior-high-age young people; provision will be made for care of the younger children, if necessary.

* Make two calls to each household as scheduled on the stewardship calendar; attempt to get an acceptance on the first call. Use the second call as a reminder and to offer or clarify any additional details (if there is a refusal on the first call, try to leave the way open to call again in the hope that they may change their minds or plans).

* Inform everyone that no pledges will be requested or received before, during, or after the "Event." Pledging is scheduled for Commitment Sunday.

* Express your own enthusiasm . . . . IT'S CONTAGIOUS!

* Please report the results of your calls to the Coordinator after each series.

Suggested Agenda for "The Event"

Social Hour and Meal	1-1/2 hours
Entertainment, if available	15 to 30 minutes
First Speaker—Senior Warden (Speaks on behalf of the Vestry; expresses support for the program; introduces and thanks the Stewardship Chairperson)	5 minutes
Second Speaker—Stewardship Chairperson (Briefly reviews the year-round program, introduces and thanks the Stewardship Committee members, and offers some thoughts about Christian Stewardship)	15 minutes
Third speaker—Commitment Coordinator (Refers to the brochure, reviews the Percentage Goal, reviews the schedule for Commitment Sunday)	10 minutes
Fourth Speaker—Parishioner (What the Christian Faith, the Church, and Christian Stewardship mean to him or her, personally)	15 minutes
Rector/Vicar—Closing prayers, Blessing	

A Sample Rector's or Vicar's Letter

(Letterhead)

(Date)

Dear (personalized),

If it were possible, I would visit each of the homes within the parish membership before Commitment Sunday to have an opportunity to discuss Christian commitment in person. This note will have to be the substitute.

You have already heard some things about the mission of the church and the Vestry's (Bishop's Committee's) goal for this year's pledging. I want to add a spiritual dimension from my particular position as your pastor.

I believe in God. I know him as Creator, Redeemer, and Sanctifier, or Father, Son, and Holy Spirit. In spite of my faults I am grateful to Him for who I am and for what I have. My life and all that sustains it is a gift from God and a reflection of His love. There are, of course, difficult times and bad moments, many due to my own shortcomings, while others are beyond anyone's control. But God is always present, and His grace prevails, and light, once again, overcomes the darkness.

When I think about my personal stewardship of my life and all that I possess, and my motive in trying to be a good steward, the only word that seems to fit is "gratitude." Being the best kind of steward that I know how to be is one way of saying "thanks" to God, and STEWARDSHIP becomes an attitude, more than the variety of offerings which serve as its manifestations.

I hope that you will think on these things, and when the time comes within a few days for you to make a commitment of a tangible sort, your pledge will reflect the intangibles of faith, which you and I share.

Thanks for sharing these moments with me.

Faithfully,

Commitment Sunday

* Publicized throughout the year, asking everyone to plan to be at one of the regular services on that day;

* Not necessarily the occasion for a "Stewardship Sermon," since the clergy are encouraged to look for stewardship themes in lessons and preaching throughout the year;

* The Stewardship Committee's plans for receiving parishioners' Commitment Cards are reviewed by the Commitment Coordinator or some other member of the Commitment Subcommittee at each of the services;

* Either of the following plans for Commitment Sunday have proved to be effective.

"Plan A" *(Parish-Wide Visitation)*

Step 1. Commissioning of all Contact Persons at the last service of the morning;

Step 2. A luncheon meeting for the Stewardship Committee, Team Captains, and all Contact Persons for purpose of receiving final instructions related to their work, team assignments, and calling lists, and for submitting personal Commitment Cards before leaving to begin making visits;

Step 3. Parish Visitation:
2:00 - 6:00 PM,	Visiting period
7:30 - 9:00 PM	Continuation of visiting and/or call back
9:00 PM	REPORT MEETING, attended by all Contact Persons, Team Captains, and Stewardship Committee members, for a report of current results, sharing of experiences, and redistribution of remaining calls, as desired

Step 4. Completion of contacts during the following week.

"Plan B" *(Limited Parish Contacts)*

Step 1. Arrangements made for Contact Persons to be present in parish hall, or some alternative location, after each of the morning services with Commitment Cards arranged in alphabetical groupings;

Step 2. Commissioning of Contact Persons takes place at the service which precedes their parish-hall assignment;

Step 3. Same as Step 2 in Plan A, after having received as many cards as possible after the services;

Step 4. Completion of contacts during the following week.

A "CLEANUP" PERIOD FOLLOWS EITHER PLAN. Having received as many commitments as possible on Commitment Sunday, the Commitment Subcommittee (Team Captains and Contact Persons) and the Stewardship Committee begin the process of completing all of the contacts. The work begins on the Monday following Commitment Sunday.

Telephone calls are made to any members of the church from whom a response has not yet been received. A "response" is a firm "yes" or "no" in regard to a commitment for the following year. The commitment is evidenced, ordinarily, by a signed Commitment Card. Such cards are not considered to be legal contracts, but rather are accepted as statements of intention (which can be altered at any time in the course of the year), giving church governing boards an indication of the resources which will probably be available.

The primary purpose of the call is arrangment of an appointment between the worker and the member. Such a meeting provides one more opportunity to offer the broad understanding of Christian Stewardship which has been emphasized throughout the year. The worker can also answer any questions the parishioner may have, clarify procedures, and receiving a Commitment Card.

Two specific sentences, included in the initial telephone conversation, are essential: "We have been asked to complete all of the contacts by next Sunday," and, "Could we meet at (date, time, and place)," negotiating the appointment from that kind of start. The first sentence is used instead of saying something like "we have been asked to get all the cards (or commitments, or pledges) in by next Sunday," since such a statement places the person in a position of having to make a decision immediately whether or not to make a commitment. The second sentence indicates that the caller is really serious about wanting to have a meeting.

Some contacts are completed in the course of the telephone call: 1) The church member may decline to make a commitment. The caller does not try to change the person's mind, but instead says that the card will be turned in and marked accordingly. 2) Someone may want more time. The caller says that he or she will call again. 3) Occasionally, the member will ask if a commitment may be made over the telephone. The caller accepts the commitment, and reports it as part of a completed contact, but commitments are never solicited by telephone.

Appointments are sometimes arranged and then not fulfilled. There can be a variety of reasons. None of them is questioned. The caller simply repeats the process in the following week. If after the caller has made two attempts to set a meeting, having actually talked to the member both times, and the effort has not been successful, the caller makes one more call, notifying the member that the card will be turned into the church office and that he or she may complete the card there. It is also made clear that any cards which are still incomplete at the end of the year are automatically considered to be indicative of no commitment for the coming year. (It is important to avoid overworking the Contact Persons. It is also important to have the definite termination point for the year's program.)

REPORTING AND MONITORING: The final report of the commitments of time and talent, as well as treasure, is prepared after the December 31 closure date. An analysis of the changes in financial commitments will assist in the evaluation of the past year's program and the planning for the coming year.

Parishes are urged to provide at least one box of offering envelopes for each household, facilitating payments from pledgers and encouraging contributions from non-pledgers as well.

A letter of acknowledgment, regular statements, and pledge and payment analyses (described in the following pages) will help to maximize fulfillment of financial commitments.

Budgeting and pledge accounting will be more accurate if the "Pledge Income" category in the parish budget is subdivided into "Previous Year's Pledges," reflecting the amount still due at the end of the year, "Current Year's Pledges," indicating the total amount pledged by the end of the year, and "Mid-year Pledges," showing an estimate of the amount expected in additional pledges during the year. A mini-program for the purpose of contracting newcomers and other selected non-pledgers is often scheduled in June to receive commitments for the final six months of the year (see appendix).

All pledge accounting is based on signed pledge cards. Contributions received in other forms, unpledged offerings, special gifts, etc., are recorded in other sections of the financial reports.

Reporting Financial Commitments

* Financial Commitment Report Form #1 may be used to record financial pledges in annual amounts as cards are received; a preliminary report is presented during the Report Meeting (Plan A), or at the meeting of Contact Persons following the Commitment Sunday pledging (Plan B);

* A final report is based on cards completed by "close of business" December 31 of the program year;

* The columns of Form #1 are used as follows:

  1. Complete parish membership list (family and individual household units, or all baptized persons, 16 years and older);

  2. Current annual pledge made by unit or individual;

  3. Annual pledge for the coming year;

  4. Using Columns 4, 5, 6, 7, 8, 9, 10: An "X" in the appropriate column indicates the classification of the response.

* The number of pledges in each category is determined by counting the "X"s in each column. The annual dollar amounts for each category are calculated by totaling the pledges corresponding to the respective "X"s.

Financial Commitment Report Form #1 *(Illustration)*

1 Names	2 Current Year	3 Next Year	4 Incr.	5 Decr.	6 New	7 Same	8 Dis-cont'd	9 None, 2 Yrs	10 No Contact
A	900	1,200	X						
	None	800			X				
	500	None						X	
	750	600		X					
	1,000	1,000				X			
	None	None						X	
B	300								X

Financial Commitment Report Form #1

1 Names	2 Current Year	3 Next Year	4 Incr.	5 Decr.	6 New	7 Same	8 Dis-cont'd	9 None, 2 Yrs	10 No Contact

Summarizing Financial Commitments

* Financial Commitment Report Form #2 offers a recapitulation of commitments completed by December 31 of the program year;

* Copies of the form are mailed to the parish membership list as a final report, and the total amount pledged for the new year is included in the new parish budget;

* The total number of units shown on Form #2 is the same as on Form #1, with all accounted for in one column or another.

Financial Commitment Report Form #2 *(Illustration)*

Pledge Category	No. of Families	Amount Current Year	Amount New Year	Change +/(-)
New	10	None	15,000	15,000
Increased	65	65,000	74,000	9,000
Same	40	45,000	45,000	–
Decreased	15	12,000	10,000	<2,000>
Subtotal	130	122,000	144,000	22,000
Discontinued	5	3,000	None	<3,000>
None, 2 yrs.	9	None	None	–
Not contacted	6	400	None	<400>
Total	150	125,400	144,000	18,600

Financial Commitment Report Form #2

Pledge Category	No. of Families	Amount Current Year	Amount New Year	Change +/(-)
New				
Increased				
Same				
Decreased				
Subtotal				
Discontinued				
None, 2 yrs.				
Not contacted				
Total				

A Sample Letter of Appreciation and Verification

(To arrive between Christmas and New Year's Eve)

(Letterhead)

(Date)

Dear

     Thank you for your ___(year)__ financial commitment to ___(name)__ Parish. Contacts are now completed and the results are being tabulated. A full report will be available after the first of the year.

     According to our records, your total financial pledge for the coming year is _____ , payable at _____ / week, _____ / month, _____ / year. If this is not correct, please notify the parish office as soon as possible.

     Offering envelopes will be available at the back of the church beginning Sunday, ____(date)____. The number on the envelope is a means of recording your contributions.

                                              Sincerely,

                              _____

                              Financial Secretary

P.S. Several of our people have asked for current pledge figures.

        Your Operating Fund Pledge was: _____

        You have paid: _____

        The balance due, 12/31/___: _____

A Sample Letter for Non-Pledging Households

(To arrive between Christmas and New Year's Eve)

(Letterhead)

(Date)

Dear

Now that we are nearing the end of another year of parish life, we want to thank everyone who has shared that life with us. It is the prayers and support and participation of all of our people which enables our church to be the Body of Christ in this place. We do appreciate your being a part of it.

This is also the time of the year when we verify our financial records, as we close this year's books and prepare for next year's budget.

We do not have a financial pledge recorded for you for the coming year, but please be assured that whatever financial support you will be able to offer will be appreciated. Offering envelopes will be available in the back of the church beginning Sunday, _____(date)_____ , for all households. The number on the envelope is our means of recording your contributions.

Again, thanks for being a part of this church.

Sincerely,

_____
Financial Secretary

(Note: Add "P.S." from pledging letter, if there was a pledge in the previous year.)

49

Monitoring Financial Commitments Through the Year

* An important step toward insuring maximum collection levels;

* Ideally, quarterly statements are mailed to all parish households, whether they have a pledge or not; (persons who are in arrears may receive monthly statements until payments are current)

* A monthly Treasurer's report to the Vestry or Bishop's Committee may include the total pledge-payment delinquency as an "Account Receivable," until some adjustment is made;

* A quarterly analysis of pledge payments (Form #3) will assist the Stewardship Committee in the identification of those pledges which may need attention, and which may also be first indications of pastoral problems or parishioner complaints;

* Analysis of pledges in the course of the year is part of the responsible management of the financial affairs of the church;

* The analysis enables monitors to focus efforts where attention is needed, rather than alarming the entire congregation;

* Any pledges which are more than one month in arrears usually should be reviewed. Closer examination will indicate whether or not the pledger should be contacted. If a contact is to be made, a pastoral attitude is indicated. It is assumed that pledges have been made in good faith, and that if payments are in arrears there may be a problem which needs attention.

Financial Commitment Report Form #3 *(Illustration)*

(Indicate category with an *X* for each family or individual)

Family Names	Paid in Advance	Current	No. Weeks Past Due			
			1 - 4	5 - 7	8 - 13	13 +
A	*X*					
			X			
					X	
B		*X*	*X*			*X*

Financial Commitment Report Form #3

Family Names	Paid in Advance	Current	No. Weeks Past Due			
			1 - 4	5 - 7	8 - 13	13 +
Total						

Parochial Stewardship Program Summary

Year _____

Name of Church _____ Address _____

City_____ County _____ Zip_____

1.   Please check which, if any, of the following parts of a "year-round" program were utilized:

        _____Information Process

        _____Long-Range Planning Process

        _____Parish Planning Conference

        _____"Percentage Goal"

        _____Local Brochure

        _____Parish-wide communications:

            _____Newsletters

            _____Sunday bulletins

            _____Senior Warden's letter

            _____Stewardship Chairperson's letter

            _____Rector's letter

            _____Other (Please describe _____)

        _____Contact-person recruiting and training

        _____Parish "Event" (e.g. Stewardship Dinner, Lunch, etc.)

        _____Commitment solicitation: (Please check method utilized)

            _____Home visitation for each household

            _____Commitment Sunday with pledges being received at the church and canvassers contacting the remaining prospects

            _____Commitment Sunday with no follow-up

            _____Mailing of pledge cards to all households, followed by contact of those not returning cards

            _____Mailing of cards with no follow-up

            _____Other (Please describe_____)

        _____Review, evaluation and planning for the next year

2.   Present number of parish households _____.

3.   Present number of pledges _____.

4.   Total annual amount pledged for the next year $_____.

APPENDICES

CONTENTS:

- A Mid-Year Review Program
- A Word About Capital Funds Drives
- Planned-Giving Programs
- An Illustration of a Space-Usage Study for Parish Buildings
- A Sample MBO for a Church, "Church Program and Administration Guide"

A Mid-Year Review Program

The ordinary year-round stewardship program is considered to be completed on December 31. The total dollar amount indicated in signed Commitment Cards as of that date is used in constructing the church budget for the coming year. Time and talent pledges also are reviewed and referred to the appropriate individuals or organizations for implementation. A final report, based on the year-round results, completes the work of the Stewardship Committee for the year.

However, as the new year begins, churches often will have uncompleted contacts carrying over from the previous year's program, as well as new families or individuals entering the congregation. Rather than continuing any effort to complete contacts which remain from the previous year, and instead of attempting to introduce newcomers to the stewardship program of the parish on an individual basis, a mid-year review process (end of first quarter *and* mid-year in a fast-growing church) has been shown to be most effective.

By the end of May (or February), the Stewardship Committee lists all uncompleted contacts and new household units as a prospect list. A mini-version of the usual fall schedule is arranged for June or March. Telephone contacts are made. An informal supper or brunch for the whole congregation is scheduled, and a letter announcing the event is mailed to the whole church, including the newcomers. The purpose of the gathering is to review the life and work of the church, at the present time, and to teach the meaning of Christian Stewardship as it applies or is reflected in the daily life of the congregation. The proportionate giving of time and talent and treasure is presented as an offering of ourselves to the role of caretaker of God's Creation through God's Church, and in other ways as well.

The Sunday following the brunch or supper is a Commitment Sunday for anyone who has not made a formal commitment for the current year. Financial pledges made during March become effective April 1 for the balance of the year. June pledges begin July 1, also for the balance of the year. Meanwhile, the entire parish is involved in the annual planning process and the activities of the fall months.

Families or individuals who have not made a commitment on the March or June Commitment Sunday are contacted within the following week by Contact Persons from the previous fall program. The Stewardship Committee issues a final report as of March 31 and/or June 30.

A Mid-Year Review Program offers an organized approach and accords an opportunity to create some momentum for the effort.

If new members of the church request Commitment Cards and/or offering envelopes, prior to being involved in a review program, they can be accommodated. However, some effort should still be made to introduce them to the church's understanding of Christian Stewardship and its development within the local congregation.

A Word About Capital Funds Drives . . .

From time to time, parishes and other institutions will discern a need for funds which will be received in addition to the proceeds of the regular annual giving programs. Such funds are used for a variety of purposes. There may be a need for the purchase or construction of new buildings. An organ or a boiler, or some other major piece of equipment, may need replacement or repair. There may be a desire to create new or additional endowment funds for future maintenance or other purposes. Whatever the particular need or needs may be, it is assumed that they cannot be met through routine programs, and a special effort is required.

Capital funds campaigns are usually directed by organizations or individuals who specialize in such projects. Charges for their services are on a fee basis, representing the amount of time and expenses which they expect to incur. The costs are established prior to the campaign. Setting the fee on the basis of a certain percentage of the dollar results of the campaign is not considered to be an ethical procedure by many of the professionals in the field.

Capital campaigns have achieved favorable results when conducted concurrently with annual-giving solicitations, or when scheduled as entirely separate programs at other times during the year. Careful preparations and management are essential in either case.

It is preferable to establish campaign goals on the basis of "potential" rather than "needs." Since such programs cannot be conducted too often, it seems reasonable to direct the effort toward maximum results. Goals based on the potential of the organization are set by the use of various formulae and an analysis of the circumstances of the individual parish.

Planned-Giving Programs . . .

Christian Stewardship involves the responsible use of all of our time and talents and treasure throughout our lives. The "3 Ts" are symbols of who we are, and they are really offerings of ourselves, our souls and bodies, for the continuation of Christ's mission and ministry, as we are enable to do so through His Church and in many other ways.

The stewardship of our financial resources involves annual giving, the occasional capital funds drive, and the possibility of a personal planned-giving program.

"Planned giving" has been defined as "the stewardship of our accumulated assets." Gifts arranged through such programs will include such things as "Charitable Gift Annuities," "Charitable Trusts," "Life Estate Contracts," gifts of life insurance, wills, and contributions offered through "The Episcopal Church Foundation Pooled Income Fund" or similar programs within individual dioceses.

Planned-giving programs at the parochial or diocesan level usually involve presentations made to parish or other audiences, raising the consciousness in regard to such possibilities, and referring interested parties to their own attorneys or accountants for implementation. A variety of printed materials, describing each of the forms of deferred gifts, is available in the diocesan resource centers.

C HURCH-OWNED BUILDINGS are often used by other groups—occasionally or on a regular basis. Most such groups are usually expected to make a financial contribution for the use of the space. Church leaders who are responsible for the financial management of the church often wonder about the amount of the contribution.

A "Space-Usage Study," as illustrated on the following page, is one way to determine a fair-share gift. In theory the study will reflect the proportionate cost for all of the use of the space by the church, as well as by the other groups.

Whether or not the leadership of the church chooses to have all groups contribute the calculated amount, the proportionate expense related to the usage by the non-church groups will be known and can be taken into account in evaluating the mission of the congregation.

Space-usage studies should be recalculated each year, as expenses and usage will vary from time to time and affect the "square-foot-hour" factor.

Space-Usage Study

(Example)

Space No.	Space Description	Length	Width	Sq. ft.	Usage Hrs/wk	No. of weeks	Annual sq.ft.hrs.	Cost @.00216
1	Rector's office	10	12	120	40	52	249,600	539.14
2	Meeting room:	17	28	476				
	Mon.—AA			476	3	52	74,256	160.39
	Tues.—Vestry			476	.5	52	12,376	26.73
	Wed.—Bible class			476	1	52	24,752	53.46
	Alateen			476	3	52	74,256	160.39
	Thur.—Lit. Guild			476	1.5	52	37,128	80.20
	Fri.—AA			476	3	52	74,256	160.39
	Sun.—Church School			476	1	52	24,752	53.46
	Emotions Anon.			476	3	52	74,256	160.39
3	Secty's office	8	10	80	24	52	99,840	215.65
4	Counseling room	15	21	315	None	None	None	None
5	Basement room	16	26	416	50	52	1,081,600	2,336.26
6	Parish hall	42	45	1,890				
	Day-care center			1,890	50	52	4,914,000	10,625.04
	Parish usage			1,890	3	52	294,840	636.85
7	Parish kitchen	12	18	216	50	52	561,600	1,213.06
8	Choir room	14	24	336				
	Choir rehearsals			336	2	52	34,944	75.48
	Music lessons			336	15	52	262,080	566.09
9	Thrift shop	14	30	420	40	52	873,600	1,886.98
10	Shop storage	14	18	252	40	52	524,160	1,132.19
11	Nursery Sch.- hall	22	45	990	40	52	2,059,200	4,447.87
12	Nursery Sch.-rm	15	38	570	40	52	1,185,600	2,560.90
13	Nursery Sch.-rm	12	34	408	40	52	848,640	1,833.06
14	Church	30	55	1,650	6	52	514,800	1,111.97

TOTALS..13,900,536 $30,035.95

Utilities, Insurance, Repairs, Maintenance, $30,030 = $.00216/sq. ft. hr.
Annual Square-Foot Hours, 13,900,536

Note: Forty hours per week represents "full-time" usage; the activities in this example happen to be weekly through the whole year, but this is not usually the case. The number of weeks included in the calculations will vary from parish to parish in respect to various activities.

MANAGEMENT BY OBJECTIVES. During the 1950s and 1960s, a large number of businesses and industries, both in the United States and overseas, began utilizing a new system of planning and implementation. Originated by Peter Drucker, a well-known business consultant and teacher, it was called "Management by Objectives" or MBO. Such an approach has proved to be useful in non-profit social-work agencies, schools, and other organizations, as well as in the business community. Offering an opportunity for an organized study and presentation of objectives and goals and resources, both interior and exterior, the system can be utilized in the church as well.

The following document is offered as an illustration of how a congregation might use the process as a means of doing long-range planning in somewhat more detail than usual. In relation to the year-round stewardship development program, the MBO might be developed following the Parish Planning Conference in preparation for the implementation of the "tentative blueprint for the next three years."

The content of the MBO will, of course, vary from congregation to congregation, while the format may be used with any church.

A CHURCH PROGRAM

AND ADMINISTRATION GUIDE

A Sample MBO

David W. Gordon

Parish Program and Administration Guide

(Example)

Goal 1. To nurture corporate and private worship for clergy and laity.

      Comment: This is the "heart of the matter," our primary reason for existence and our most appropriate response to God's love for us. It is no more automatic for the clergy than for the laity. All need help and encouragement in accordance with individual levels of development in the faith. All are capable of creating and maintaining good habits of corporate and individual prayer, if offered proper guidance and support.

    Objective A. To provide a complete schedule of services in the tradition of the Church.

        Section 1.   To provide the Holy Eucharist as the principal service each Sunday.

        Section 2.   To provide the Daily Office Monday through Saturday.

        Section 3.   To provide an observance of the Saints' Days and Holy Days with at least one celebration of the Holy Eucharist.

        Section 4.   To initiate a daily celebration of the Holy Eucharist as soon as possible.

        Section 5.   To encourage increased utilization of the "occasional services" as appropriate.

    Objective B. To have worship experiences which are truly meaningful, while varying style and content.

        Section 1.   To utilize the variety of options in the *Book of Common Prayer* as they pertain to all of the services.

        Section 2.   To introduce new service music and hymns as they become available, with proper preparation for all participants.

        Section 3.   To recognize and accommodate developmental levels of laity of all ages to the greatest extent possible.

        Section 4.   To use alternative approaches to traditional homiletics.

        Section 5.   To provide for feedback, constructive criticism, or evaluation as a means of "quality control".

    Objective C. To assure that all services are conducted with good liturgical style.

        Section 1.   To have adequate instruction, training, and rehearsal for all participants.

        a. Weekly acolyte team training and one monthly meeting for all acolytes.

        b. Monthly Altar Guild meetings and at least two field trips each year for the entire Guild.

c. Weekly two-hour choir rehearsals for each choir, plus a firteen-minute "warm-up" period on Sunday morning.

d. Training sessions for ushers at least three times per year.

e. Meetings for lay readers and lectors at least three times per year.

Section 2. To assure proper vestments for all participants.

Section 3. To maintain orderly and clean appointments and careful preparations by the Altar Guild.

Section 4. To maintain a clean, comfortable, and attractive setting with a devotional and hospitable atmosphere for all services.

Re: Objectives A, B, and C

Internal Resources: One priest, five licensed lay readers, four cupbearers, three lectors, 24 Altar Guild members, 16 acolytes, one organist/choir director, ushers an attractive, well-appointed and well-equipped church building and chapel, memorial funds.

Internal Restraints: An incomplete organ, needing repair, voicing, tuning, expansion; underdeveloped choir potential; shortage of clergy assistance in and for services; noise problems from organ and furnaces; lack of regular custodial work; absence of narthex for temperature and sound control; lack of proper access space within church loft for full utilization; small book racks and inadequate book supply; traditional architecture versus modern liturgy.

External Resources: Diocesan and seminary workshops in liturgics and music; available consultation; continuing education for clergy and laity through church and community; diocesan training program for auxiliary clergy; diocesan lay reader training guidelines and resources; articles in magazines and books.

External Restraints: None. (Comment: There is nothing outside the parish congregation which can restrain them from having a meaningful worship experience at their own levels.)

Goal 2. To develop a program of Christian education for children, youth, and adults.

Comment: "Faith is caught, not taught," but faith must also be nurtured with content and understanding and relevancy to the Christian's daily life. Continuing Christian education is essential for parishioners of all ages as a means of lifelong personal and spiritual growth.

Objective A. To provide a program of adult education, sound in content and relevant to daily living, presented in a well-prepared and attractive variety of approaches or styles.

Section 1. To provide at least one weekly adult Bible class at the church on Sunday morning.

Section 2. To organize a maximum of six weekly Bible-study groups in homes on week nights.

Section 3. To schedule one six-week Wednesday-evening course in the fall and one during Lent.

Section 4. To recruit and train two lay readers for each home Bible-study group.

Section 5. To invite prominent and qualified leadership from outside the parish for the two or three six-week courses.

Section 6. To insert forums in the Sunday-morning Bible-class time as needed

Section 7. To encourage attendance at lectures, conferences, workshops, etc., as offered by church and community.

Section 8. To conduct at least one series of Inquirer's Classes each year.

Objective B. To provide a program for youth, including aspects of worship, study, service, and fellowship.

Section 1. To establish a weekly class for senior high school students.

Section 2. To establish a monthly E.Y.C. meeting for purposes of planning and administration.

Section 3. To schedule one monthly "workday" for parish or nonparochial projects.

Section 4. To schedule one major social event for parish high school students and their friends each month.

Section 5. To schedule one annual weekend retreat away from the parish.

Section 6. To maximize youth participation in the corporate worship of the parish, and to encourage development of personal "rules of life" for family and personal devotions.

Section 7. To recruit and train one man and one woman to be advisors in the youth program.

Section 8. To establish a steering committee comprised of youth, advisors, and the Rector for the purpose of planning and implementing the program as a whole.

Objective C. To organize and maintain a church-school program for children who are from three years of age through the eighth grade.

Section 1. To establish a curriculum review and advisory committee of three lay persons.

Section 2. To establish a parent's group, responsible for arrangements (classroom, transportation, special equipment, supplies, etc.).

Section 3. To recruit and train teachers and assistants as required.

Section 4. To utilize extra-parochial resources in personnel and materials.

Section 5. To foster attendance and participation in church and community workshops, etc.

Section 6. To schedule major events for church-school pupils of all ages.

Re: Objective A

Internal Resources: One priest, one candidate for Holy Orders, active and retired teachers, and other interested laity; an extensive parish library; adequate facilities and equipment.

Internal Restraints: Time required for other pastoral and administrative responsibilities limits Rector's time available for proper preparation; time limits for laity as well; low participant numbers limit leadership motivation; potential lay leadership feelings of inadequacy.

External Resources: Speakers, leaders, et al. available through diocese, seminary, community; diocesan A/V library; adult study courses from a variety of denominations; denominational and ecumenical leadership-training resources.

External Restraints: None

Re: Objective B and C

Internal Resources: Same as for Objective A

Internal Restraints: Children and youth are engaged in many and varied activities in school and community, limiting time and interest for church program; reluctance of qualified laity to assume teaching and administrative responsibilities; lack of strong parental support; negative church school experience in children's, youths' and parents' past church life; reluctance of parents and teachers to accept changes in principles and practices of good pedagogy; confusion in understanding similarities and differences vis-à-vis worship and education.

External Resources: Same as for Objective A.

External Restraints: Negative influence from peer groups; secular-minded community; apathy and/or hostility from adult associates; dubious image of Episcopal Church per press, TV, etc., inhibits interest and growth potential among unchurched.

Goal 3. To mobilize and motivate the parish membership in a program of church growth.

Comment: The Christian has a dual responsibility "to know Christ and to make Him known." Our personal knowledge and experience of faith grows through prayer and study and in our associations with fellow Christians. We then share this faith with others in fulfillment of Jesus' "Great Commission" which directed us "to go into all the world." And as we share with others through word and action, our own faith is made even stronger.

Objective A. To establish an organized church-growth program.

Section 1. To establish a Church Growth Steering Committee of six people.

Section 2. To enlist twenty-four "callers."

Section 3.   To schedule a parish Church Growth Seminar with an attendance of at least 36 parishioners.

Section 4.   To establish specific growth goals for the next five years.

Objective B. To develop a working zone system as an adjunct to the church-growth program.

Section 1.   To appoint, organize, and instruct 12 zone chairmen.

Section 2.   To schedule six home meetings in the fall.

Section 3.   To assign members of the vestry to each zone and to define their specific responsibilities related to the zone work.

Section 4.   To utilize the zones of the parish as a means of decentralization of parish programs in worship, study, service, and fellowship, while maintaining parish-wide activities for the upbuilding of congregational corporateness.

Objective C. To maintain a warm, welcoming atmosphere in conjunction with church services and parish hall activities and throughout the zone programming.

Section 1.   To recruit, organize and train a corps of 24 ushers, scheduling two ushers for the eight o'clock service and four for the ten o'clock service each Sunday.

Section 2.   To provide continental breakfast after the eight o'clock service and a coffee hour after the ten o'clock service each Sunday.

Section 3.   To schedule an all-parish supper each month.

Section 4.   To continue the monthly luncheons for the women of the parish.

Section 5.   To establish an evening group for the women of the parish parallel to the monthly luncheon group.

Section 6.   To schedule a Saturday breakfast meeting for the men of the parish each month.

Section 7.   To utilize zone meetings for the purpose of acquainting present parishioners and welcoming newcomers.

Section 8.   To establish a "home visitor" in each zone to assist the Rector in the pastoral ministry of the parish.

Section 9.   To have a Homecoming Sunday each year, stressing attendance by former parish members.

Section 10.   To maintain a cycle of intercessory prayer in the Daily Office, and to notify by card, note, or call when the prayers are being offered.

Re: Objectives A, B, and C

Internal Resources: Rector and three laity attended a diocesan Church Growth Seminar; a number of laity indicated interest through a pre-seminar questionnaire; a good church facility in a good location.

Internal Restraints: Lay apathy with respect to growth; lay aversion to team evangelism; poor physical appearance of some parts of parish facility; limitations on maintenance equipment.

External Resources: Church-growth consultants; resource books, articles, A/V; seminars on church growth.

External Restraints: Episcopal Church image per press; secular society; time limits from extra-parochial life.

Goal 4. To foster good stewardship of time, talent, and treasure on the part of all members of the parish.

Comment: Implementation of good stewardship principles enables the congregation to fulfill its responsibilities. An understanding of stewardship theology provides a perspective for all aspects of daily life.

Objective A. To conduct an effective stewardship program each year, soliciting time, talent, and treasure pledges.

Objective B. To conduct a partial canvass of newcomers and other non-pledgers at mid-year.

Objective C. To monitor all pledges of time, talent, and/or treasure.

Objective D. To develop a program of deferred giving.

Objective E. To establish a parish endowment fund.

Objective F. To utilize volunteer time and talent as fully as possible in programming and physical maintenance of the parish.

Objective G. To develop and maintain a strong program of outreach in service to community, diocese, and national Church, utilizing time, talent, and treasure of all parishioners.

Objective H. To provide proper maintenance and repair for all parish property.

Re: Objectives A through H

Internal Resources: Past experience of Rector and laity in stewardship programs; appropriate records and materials; previous training of laity.

Internal Restraints: False sense of security leading to apathetic attitudes with respect to finances; time limitations for potential lay leadership and for lay stewardship of time and talent in general; slow prioritizing of individual resources.

External Resources: Diocesan and national consultation, resources, and supplies.

External Restraints: Hedonistic and materialistic society.

Goal 5. To provide the resources in personnel, equipment, and supplies for the effective implementation of the parish goals.

      Comment: No person or parish can function properly if inadequately staffed and equipped. Creativity and morale are both stifled. The volume of work produced is limited. Human resources are not utilized to full potential when occupied with inappropriate activities.

Objective A. The employment of a part-time, qualified organist-choir director.

Objective B. The employment of a part-time parish secretary.

Objective C. The recruitment, organization, and training of five volunteer office workers to supplement the work of the parish secretary.

Objective D. The appointment of a volunteer administrative assistant to work with the Rector in the program and business administration of the parish.

Objective E. To employ a part-time parish sexton and groundskeeper.

Objective F. To secure seminarian assistance through the Field Education Program of the seminary with special assignment in youth ministries.

Objective G. To accomplish the following purchases as quickly as possible:

Section 1. Twelve (12) parish-hall tables.

Section 2. One hundred (100) steel chairs.

Section 3. One (1) church signboard.

Section 4. One (1) "Code-A-Phone" with remote-control attachment.